Contents

Some words are shown in bold, **like this**.
You can find out what they mean by looking
in the Glossary.

Making mountains

Some mountains began as **layers** of rock under the sea. When the earth moved, the layers were pushed up and out of the sea.

These mountains were made millions of years ago

Sand and mud fell to the bottom of the sea.

60 million years ago.

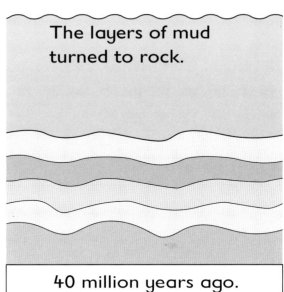

The layers of mud turned to rock.

40 million years ago.

The layers were pushed up and the sea got smaller.

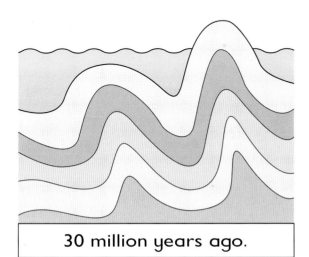

30 million years ago.

The rock was pushed into jagged shapes above the sea.

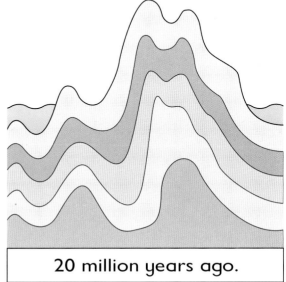

20 million years ago.

5

Volcano

A **volcano** is a mountain that is still being made. When a volcano **erupts** it blasts ash high into the sky.

This grey cloud is ash.
It is coming from a volcano

Red hot lava

The rock inside the volcano is so hot it melts. The melted rock is called **lava**. Lava is thrown out of the volcano when it erupts.

Sleeping volcanoes

When a **volcano erupts** it leaves a round hole called a crater. The crater can fill with water and make a lake.

A lake at the top of a volcano

This volcano has not erupted for a
long time. Snow covers the cold rocks

Some volcanoes are quiet for a long time.
Then they suddenly erupt. We say the
volcano has been sleeping.

Up and down

The **foothills** are the lowest part of the mountain. Soil covers the rocks so many plants can grow here.

Green fields in the foothills of a mountain

Steep slopes at the top

The top of the mountain is called the summit. The summit is often made of bare rocks.

Going up

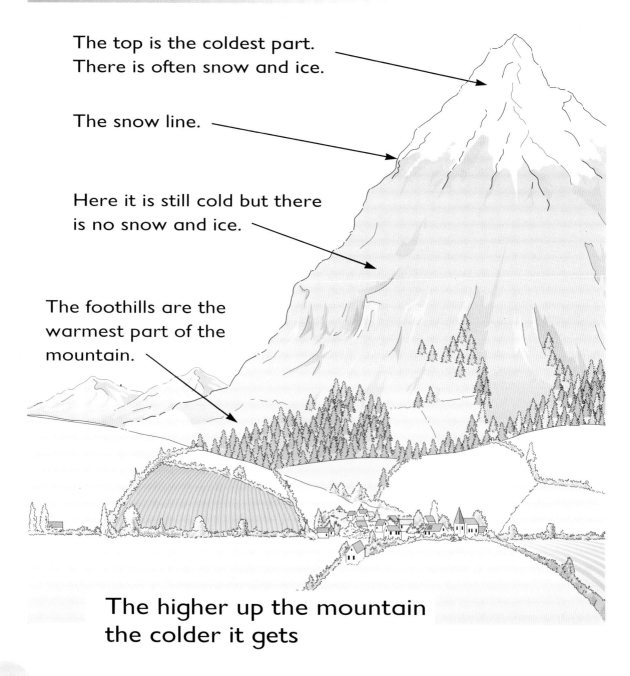

The top is the coldest part.
There is often snow and ice.

The snow line.

Here it is still cold but there
is no snow and ice.

The foothills are the
warmest part of the
mountain.

The higher up the mountain
the colder it gets

Masks make it easier to breathe on high mountains

The air has less oxygen towards the top of a tall mountain. People find it hard to breathe.

Ice on the mountain

Glaciers are rivers made of ice. It takes thousands of years for the glacier to slip down the mountain. As it moves it cuts into the rocks.

The jagged rocks above this glacier were cut by ice

This valley was made by a glacier thousands of years ago

When the ice has melted it leaves a **valley**. The steep sides and the flat bottom were made by the moving glacier.

Mountain water

As water flows down the mountain it cuts into the rock. A deep cut in the rock is called a **gorge**. It takes thousands of years for a river to cut the steep sides of a gorge.

The Grand Canyon is a large gorge with steep sides

Waterfalls cut into the mountain

Steep mountain cliffs are cut by falling water.
The mountain is slowly worn down by the
moving water.

Desert mountains

Rocks are warmed by the sun in the day. They cool down at night. This makes the rock crack and break off in **layers**.

This rock has cracked and layers have broken off it

These mountains are
slowly crumbling away

Some mountains in dry places have flat tops
and steep cliffs. In this desert, huge fingers of
rock stick out of the desert.

Falling mountains

Lots of rock can suddenly break off the mountain side. The rocks tumble and slide down. When this happens quickly it is called a **landslide**.

Landslides can block roads and trap people

Snow can suddenly fall down steep mountain slopes. This is called an **avalanche**. An avalanche grows bigger as it sweeps down the mountain.

They will destroy anything in their way

Mountain map 1

These mountains rise high above the sea. We cannot tell how high a mountain is from a photo.

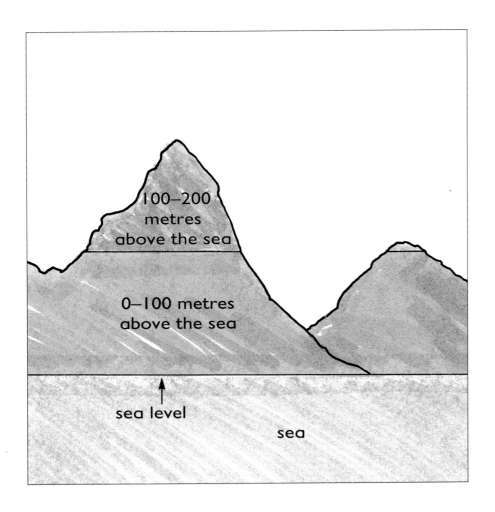

100–200
metres
above the sea

0–100 metres
above the sea

sea level

sea

The colours on this picture shows
how high the mountains are above
the sea. Maps use colours in this way
to show the height of the land.

23

Mountain map 2

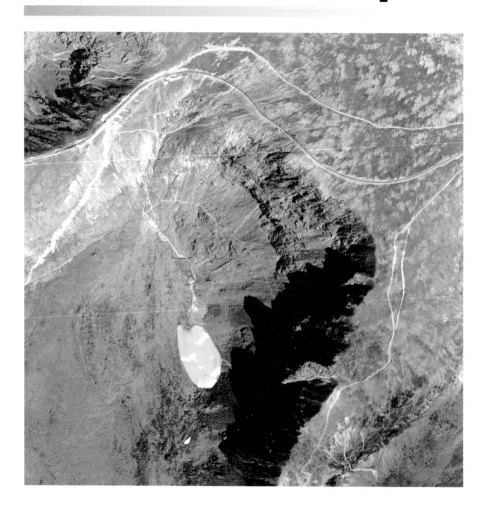

This is a photo of part of a mountain. It was taken from an aeroplane. You can see a track leading up to the top of the mountain. There is a small lake at the bottom of a steep slope.

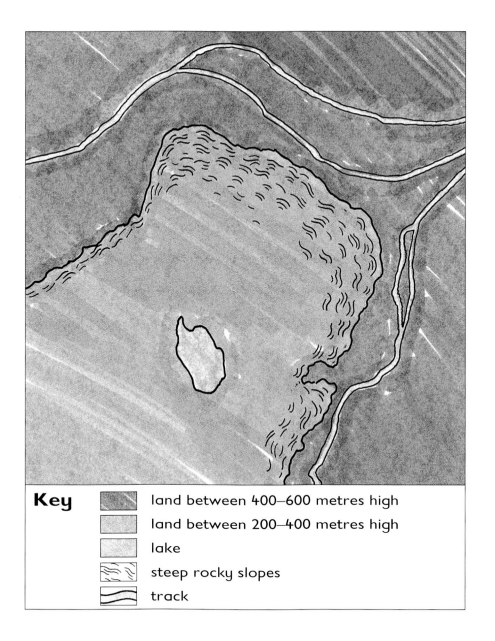

Key

▨	land between 400–600 metres high
▢	land between 200–400 metres high
▢	lake
〰	steep rocky slopes
〰	track

The purple colour shows the higher part of the mountain. The steepest rocky slopes are shown using shapes. The brown shows the lower part where there is a lake.

Mountain map 3

This photo shows another part of the same mountain. You can see steep slopes at the top of the photo. The **valley** is in the bottom of the photo. There is a river and a road in the valley.

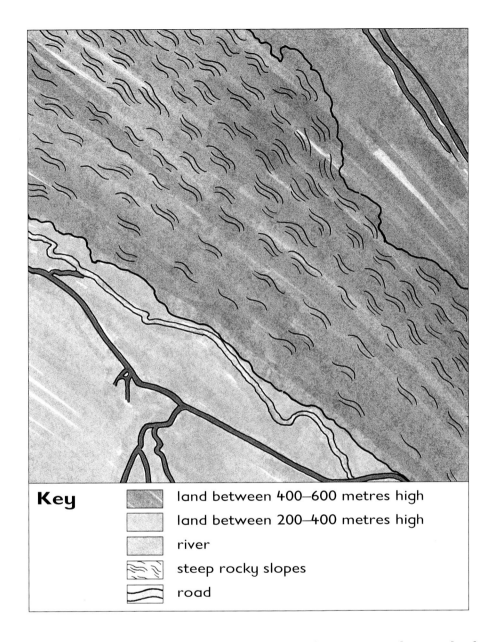

Key

▨	land between 400–600 metres high
▨	land between 200–400 metres high
▨	river
▨	steep rocky slopes
▨	road

Lines are used to show the road and the river. The road was built on flat land in the valley.

Amazing facts

Everest is the highest mountain on land. The top of Everest is 8,848 metres above the sea. The first men to climb Everest were Edmund Hillary and Tenzing Norkay in 1953.

The largest **volcano** in the world is Mauna Loa in the Pacific Ocean. It once **erupted** for one and a half years. Rivers of **lava** can flow as fast as 168 metres per second.

Glossary

avalanche   when lots of snow falls quickly from the mountain

erupts   when hot rocks burst out of a volcano

foothills   the lowest slopes of a mountain

glaciers   rivers of ice

gorge   a very steep sided valley

landslide   when rocks fall quickly from the mountain

lava   hot rocks that have melted

layers   thicknesses or levels

valley   low land between hills

volcano   a mountain made out of lava

More books to read

Nicola Baxter. *Our Wonderful Earth.*
Two-Can, 1997

Sabrina Crewe. *Step-by-Step: Hills and Mountains*
Franklin Watts, 1996

Claire Llewellyn. *Why do we have?*
Rocks and Mountains.
Heinemann, 1997

Keith Lye. *First Starts: Mountains.*
Franklin Watts, 1992

Index